She Went Out on a Limb

She Went Out on a Limb
(a book of inspiration for women)

Sandy Gingras

**Andrews McMeel
Publishing, LLC**

Kansas City • Sydney • London

Andrews McMeel Publishing, LLC
an Andrews McMeel Universal company
1130 Walnut Street, Kansas City, Missouri 64106

www.andrewsmcmeel.com
www.how-to-live.com

13 14 15 16 17 SDB 10 9 8 7 6 5 4 3 2 1

ISBN: 978-1-4494-2728-3

Library of Congress Control Number: 2012941996

ATTENTION: SCHOOLS AND BUSINESSES

Andrews McMeel books are available at quantity discounts with bulk purchase for educational, business, or sales promotional use. For information, please e-mail the Andrews McMeel Publishing Special Sales Department: specialsales@amuniversal.com

She Went Out on a Limb

One warm spring day, a woman drove up to my house in an old pickup truck with some stuff she wanted to sell me for my store. I climbed up into the bed of the truck and looked at a wonderful, worn and paint-chipped table, a green oar and a cardboard box filled with this and that. And then she showed me a big hand-painted

sign that said:
  "She went out on a limb,
   had it break off,
   and realized she could fly."
Wow, I thought!
   Instead of putting it in my
store to sell, I hung it up
over my workbench, and I
look at it every day. Some
days, when I'm scared, it
reassures me. Some days,

it affirms and encourages me. Always, it inspires me.

I wrote this book so you can open it anywhere and get a little sign of your own-- a "YES, YOU CAN!" or a "GO FOR IT!" when you need it. There's a friendly noodge on every page. I hope it helps you on your journey to become your truest, happiest and most fulfilled self.

On
going out on
a limb...

Give yourself permission

1 2 3 4 5

to grow.

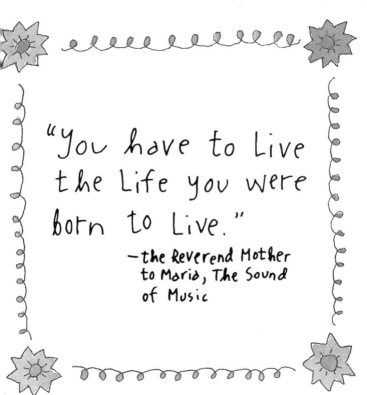

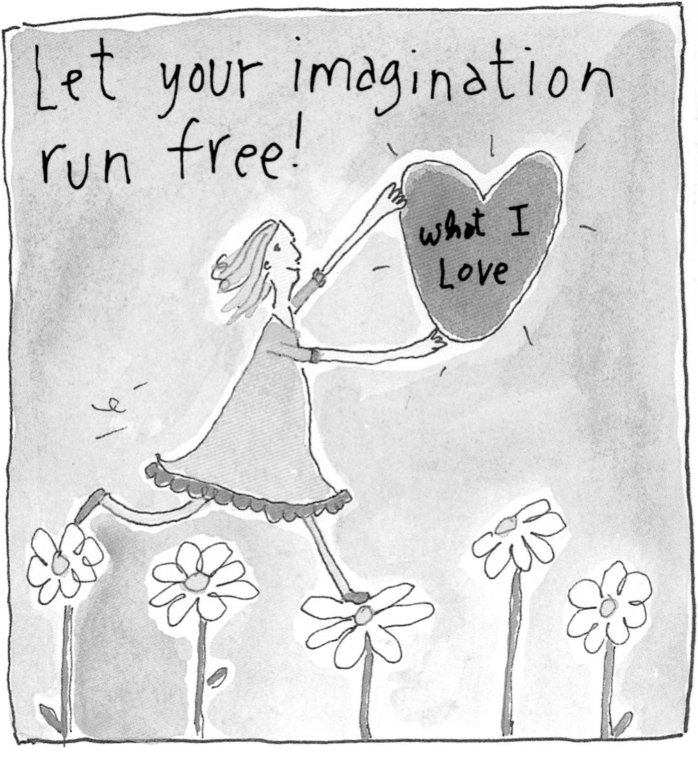
Let your imagination run free!
what I Love

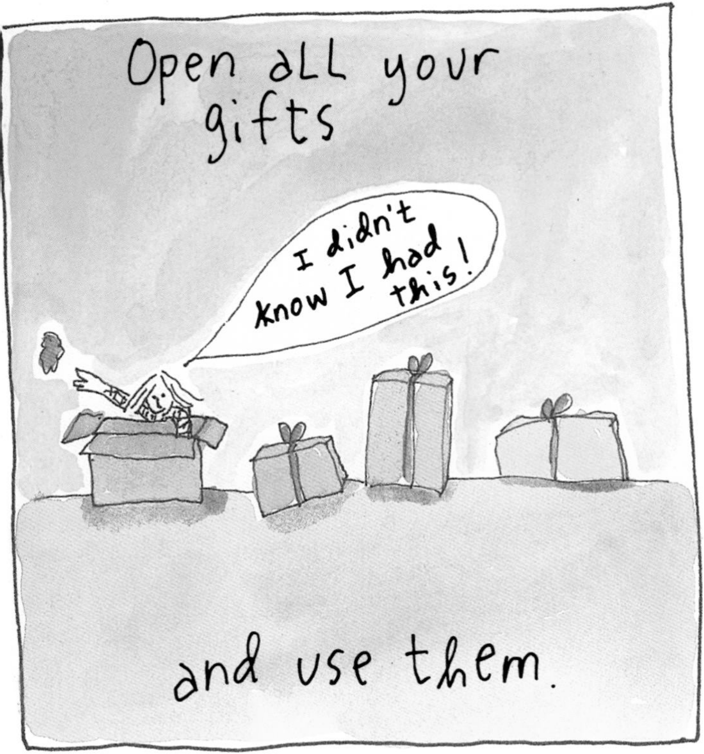
Open aLL your gifts
I didn't know I had this!
and use them.

Listen to

your inner voice.

On

fear...

Stand tall.
Be you.
Open up. This
is your time to
blossom and grow.
Believe in
yourself. Trust life.

"To the tiger
in the zoo,
Madeline just said,
'pooh-pooh.'"
—Ludwig Bemelmans

Let the butterflies in your stomach come out and play.

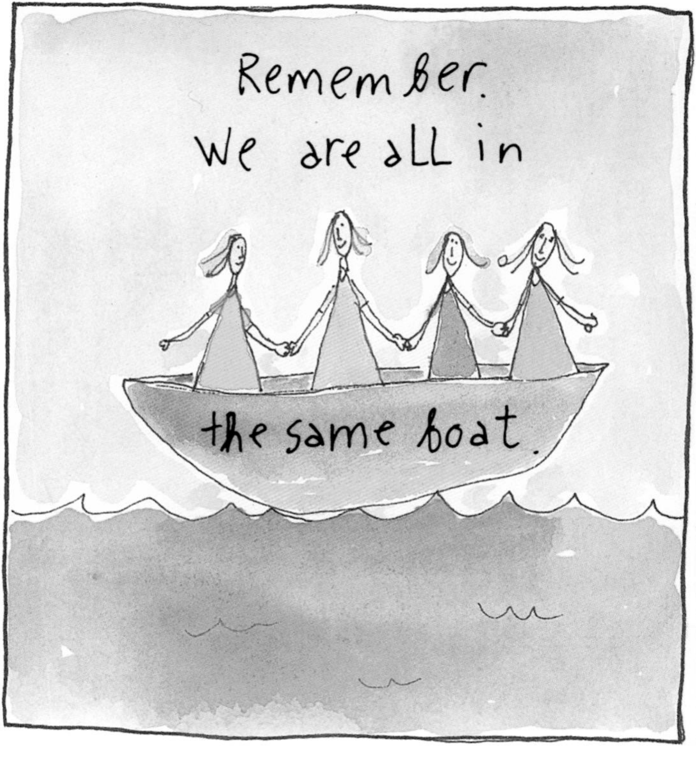
Remember.
We are all in
the same boat.

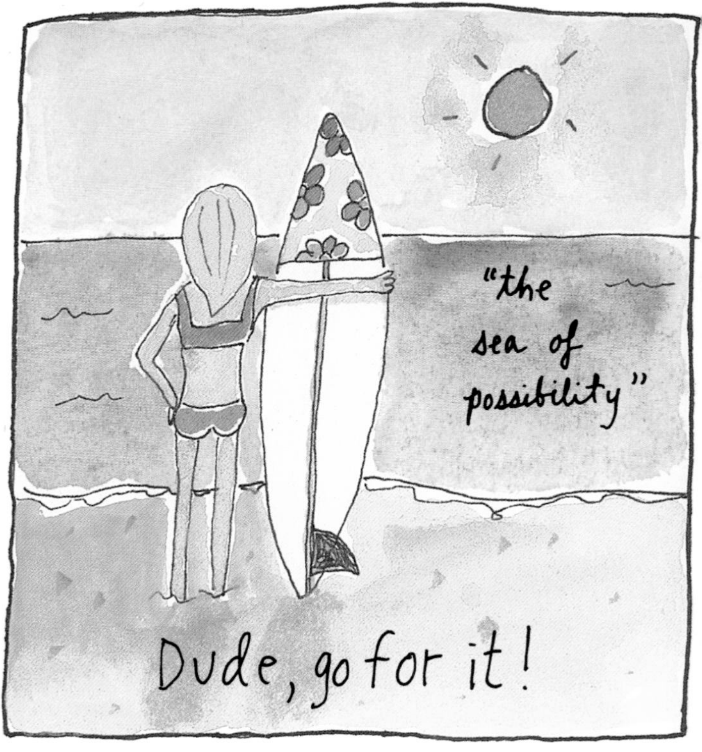
"the sea of possibility"
Dude, go for it!

"Today is a new day."
— Chicken Little

There's no such thing

as impossible.

On
procrastination...

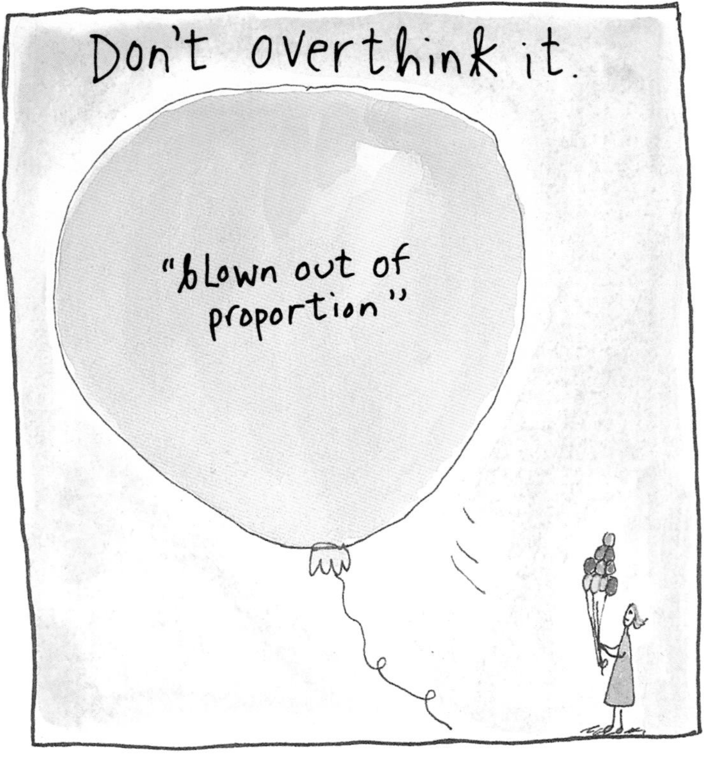
Don't overthink it.
"blown out of proportion"

One step
at a time...

Don't get all tangled up.

NOW

is your time.

On
perfectionism...

"Today, you are you, that is truer than true. There is no one alive who is you-er than you."

— Dr. Seuss

Remember that pitfalls in your path

are places to plant seeds.

Don't
value
this

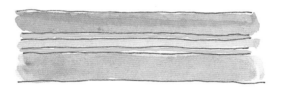

"fast and straight"

over this

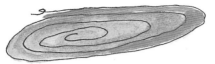

"Lost"

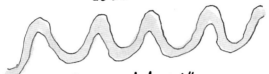

"ups and downs"

"meandering"

"Loop de Loops"

The carousel goes
'round and 'round,

and you get a second chance.

Trust your journey
you're crazy!
Go back
Beep! Beep! I'm coming through...
you can't do it.
even when nobody else does.

kick
off
your shoes

and dance.

On
rejection and criticism
and
other
obstacles...

Believe in your own
magicalness

Hope will carry you through

even the deepest water.

"The itsy bitsy spider ♫
went up the water spout.
♫ Down came the rain ♫
and washed the spider out.
Out came the sun and
dried up all the rain. ♫
♫ And the itsy bitsy spider
went up the spout again."

— children's rhyme

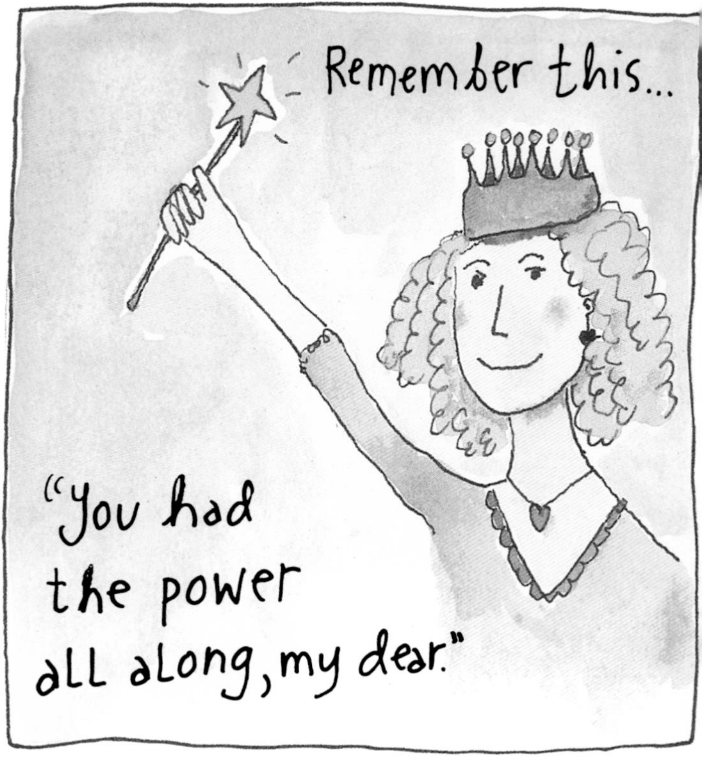
Remember this...
"You had the power all along, my dear."

LOVE your Life.

Go where no woman
has gone before,

and
make your
own beautiful
path.

She went out on a limb,
had it break off,
and realized
that she
could
fly...

Other books by Sandy Gingras